Friendship Rocks

FRIENDS ACCEPT YOU

by Megan Borgert-Spaniol

raintree
a Capstone company — publishers for children

Raintree is an imprint of Capstone Global Library Limited, a company incorporated in England and Wales having its registered office at 264 Banbury Road, Oxford, OX2 7DY – Registered company number: 6695582

www.raintree.co.uk
myorders@raintree.co.uk

Hardback edition © Capstone Global Library Limited 2023
Paperback edition © Capstone Global Library Limited 2024
The moral rights of the proprietor have been asserted.

All rights reserved. No part of this publication may be reproduced in any form or by any means (including photocopying or storing it in any medium by electronic means and whether or not transiently or incidentally to some other use of this publication) without the written permission of the copyright owner, except in accordance with the provisions of the Copyright, Designs and Patents Act 1988 or under the terms of a licence issued by the Copyright Licensing Agency, 5th Floor, Shackleton House, 4 Battle Bridge Lane, London SE1 2HX (www.cla.co.uk). Applications for the copyright owner's written permission should be addressed to the publisher.

Original illustrations © Capstone Global Library Limited 2023
Originated by Capstone Global Library Ltd

978 1 3982 4152 7 (hardback)
978 1 3982 4153 4 (paperback)

British Library Cataloguing in Publication Data
A full catalogue record for this book is available from the British Library.

Acknowledgements
We would like to thank the following for permission to reproduce photographs: Shutterstock: Brocreative, 7, Dmytro Zinkevych, 17, Karen Culp, 5, Lopolo, 10, Monkey Business Images, 19, Naypong Studio, 9, Nina Buday, 15, nito, 21, Patrick Foto, Cover, Sudowoodo, 20, wavebreakmedia, 11, worawit_j, 13.

Design elements: Mighty Media, Inc.

Every effort has been made to contact copyright holders of material reproduced in this book. Any omissions will be rectified in subsequent printings if notice is given to the publisher.

CONTENTS

Friendly dinner 4

Celebrate differences 6

Accept yourself 8

Strengths and challenges 10

Be understanding 12

Agree to disagree 14

See the best in others 16

Include others 18

    Practise acceptance 20

    Glossary 22

    Find out more 23

    Index 24

    About the author 24

Words in **bold** are in the glossary.

Friendly dinner

You **invite** your new friend to dinner. It's taco night! But your friend says she can't have the tacos. Her family does not eat meat.

You want your friend to try the food. But you accept your friend as she is. This means you don't ask her to change. You have tacos with no meat instead!

Celebrate differences

Think about a friend. How are you and your friend alike? How are you different?

You and your friend might like different sports. Maybe you have a different skin colour. These differences are good! They make us who we are.

Accept yourself

Nobody is good at everything, including you! Accepting others starts with accepting yourself. Maybe you wish you were better at drawing. But it's OK not to be perfect. You have many talents you can be proud of.

Strengths and challenges

Everyone has different strengths and **challenges**. Maybe you are good at maths. Your friend is good at spelling.

Maybe you are better at running. But your friend is better at climbing. We can be happy about our friends' strengths. We can also help them with their challenges.

Be understanding

Accepting others can be hard. You let a friend use your new colouring pencils. He breaks one. You feel angry at first. But then you decide to show **empathy**.

Empathy means understanding how someone else feels. You know your friend feels bad. He did not mean to break the pencil. You accept your friend's **apology**.

Agree to disagree

Sometimes you may disagree with a friend. Your friend likes cats. You only like dogs. It is OK to disagree. You can still be friends.

You can be kind even when you disagree. Ask your friend to tell you more about his views. Or decide to talk about things you both like.

See the best in others

Think of a time you **behaved** badly. You were not acting like your best self. But you still wanted others to show you kindness. You wanted to be accepted too.

Your friend got a bad mark on a test. Now she is being rude to you. You know she is just **upset** about the test. She needs your kindness because she is feeling down.

Include others

Accepting others means including them.
You are playing at breaktime. Your group doesn't want your classmate to play.
But you know it feels horrible to be left out.
So, you choose to be a good friend.
You invite your classmate to join in.

Practise acceptance

Sometimes we only like our own ideas. You can practise acceptance by planning a pretend trip with a friend!

 **WHAT TO DO:**

1. Imagine you are taking a trip with your friend. Let your friend pick where to go.

2. Accept your friend's trip ideas. Your friend might say, "Let's go to the beach!" Say "Yes!" or "OK!" to accept the idea.

3. Add to your friend's ideas. You could say, "Let's build a sandcastle!"

4. Draw each other's ideas to create a plan for your trip.

Glossary

apology saying sorry

behave act in a certain way

challenge something a person finds hard to do

empathy ability to understand how others feel

invite ask someone to do something or go somewhere

upset unhappy or angry

Find out more

Being a Good Friend (Mind Matters), Mari Schuh (Raintree, 2021)

Caring (Dealing with Feeling...), Isabel Thomas (Raintree, 2014)

The Same But Different, Molly Potter (Featherstone, 2021)

Index

accepting yourself 8, 16
anger 12
behaving badly 16
challenges 10, 11
differences 6, 10, 11
disagreeing 14
empathy 12
feelings 12, 16, 18
kindness 14, 16
strengths 10, 11
talents 8

About the author

Megan Borgert-Spaniol is an author and editor of children's media. When she isn't writing or reading, she enjoys doing yoga, eating croissants and crafting homemade pizzas. Megan lives in Minnesota, USA, with a tall, goofy man and a small, chatty cat.